Original title:
Friendship's Fulfillment

Copyright © 2024 Swan Charm
All rights reserved.

Author: Paula Raudsepp
ISBN HARDBACK: 978-9916-86-590-3
ISBN PAPERBACK: 978-9916-86-591-0
ISBN EBOOK: 978-9916-86-592-7

Trails of Shared Adventures

Through winding paths we roam,
Hand in hand, we find our home.
With laughter echoing in the trees,
We dance to the whispers of the breeze.

The sun sets low, casting golden hues,
Every step reveals vibrant views.
Moments woven, as stars align,
In this journey, your heart entwines.

Beneath the sky, a canvas wide,
Side by side, we take the ride.
With every trail, a story grows,
In every heartbeat, adventure flows.

Through rivers wide and mountains high,
Together, we soar, learning to fly.
As memories bloom like flowers bright,
Every sunset marks our delight.

In shadows deep, we seek the light,
With you, my world feels just right.
In trails we've walked, love's essence grows,
Forever cherished, our hearts compose.

The Essence of Togetherness

In quiet moments, we confide,
Two souls merging, side by side.
With gentle smiles, we share the day,
In your warmth, I find my way.

Laughter dances, a joyful sound,
In your presence, peace is found.
Every story, a thread we weave,
In this bond, we truly believe.

Through storms and sun, we will stand,
Building dreams, hand in hand.
With each challenge, our spirits rise,
In togetherness, the heart flies.

As seasons change, our love remains,
A steady pulse through joy and pains.
In shared glances, our truth shines bright,
Together, we chase the light.

In the tapestry of life we spin,
Each moment cherished, where love begins.
With every heartbeat, we affirm
The essence of us in every term.

When Hearts Open Wide

In quiet moments shared,
We find the light inside.
With whispers soft and true,
When hearts open wide.

Connections woven deep,
In laughter, love does thrive.
Together hand in hand,
We dance, we feel alive.

Through storms that may collide,
We gather strength anew.
With every tear we shed,
Our bond remains so true.

In every glance we share,
A story formed in time.
With hope that never fades,
Our love, a perfect rhyme.

So let the world go by,
With trust, we will abide.
In all that life may bring,
When hearts open wide.

A Tapestry of Trust

Threads of gold and blue,
We weave our dreams so bright.
In every gentle touch,
We find our guiding light.

With echoes of the past,
Each moment stitched with care.
In patterns shared with love,
A tale beyond compare.

Through trials and the joy,
Our fabric holds us tight.
In laughter, in our tears,
We shine, a beacon light.

With every story told,
The colors intertwine.
In unity, we stand,
A love that's truly fine.

So let us hold this trust,
A bond that will not sever.
In this vast tapestry,
We find our strength forever.

Harmony in Togetherness

With hands held side by side,
We paint the skies above.
In every beat we share,
We find our song of love.

Through rhythms of the heart,
Our spirits intertwine.
In harmony, we dream,
Our souls in perfect line.

When shadows dance around,
We light the darkened night.
In unity, we stand,
Our bond a source of light.

With every step we take,
We find our way with grace.
In laughter, in our tears,
Together, we embrace.

So let the music play,
In hearts, a melody.
In harmony, we grow,
Together, you and me.

Seeds of Joy

In gardens of the heart,
We plant the seeds of care.
With love as our sunlight,
Together, joy we share.

As blooms begin to rise,
In colors rich and bright.
Each petal tells a tale,
Of laughter, warmth, and light.

Through seasons of our lives,
We nurture what we've sown.
In every moment shared,
The joy has brightly grown.

In breezes soft and warm,
We dance beneath the trees.
With every whisper shared,
Our spirits find their ease.

So let us tend our dreams,
With kindness as our guide.
For in this world of ours,
Are seeds of joy inside.

Anchors in Each Other's Souls

In the depths of calm seas,
We find solace in our hearts,
Each whisper tethers our dreams,
Anchored firm, never apart.

Like stars that light the night,
Holding fast through every storm,
With love as our guiding light,
We endure, steadfast and warm.

Through shadows that may creep,
We embrace the ebb and flow,
In your eyes, I find my keep,
A strength that helps me grow.

Together, through the tides,
We navigate this vast world,
In your arms, my heart abides,
In our love, we are unfurled.

Forever we shall sail on,
With hearts forever so bold,
Waves may rise, but love is drawn,
Anchors in each other's souls.

Heartstrings Intertwined

Your laughter sings to my soul,
A melody soft and sweet,
Each note a story we share,
In harmony, we compete.

In the warmth of your embrace,
I find my refuge and peace,
Two hearts beat in rhythm's grace,
As time slows and fears release.

Moments tangled like vines,
In a garden we both tend,
Through life's chapters, we align,
Every twist a loving bend.

With every glance, a spark,
Igniting flames deep within,
In the quiet, we embark,
A journey where love begins.

Together, we weave a song,
In the fabric of our days,
With heartstrings intertwined strong,
In love's intricate displays.

A Canvas of Laughter

Painted smiles fill the air,
Colors burst like joyful streams,
With laughter, we declare,
Life's a tapestry of dreams.

Every moment, a bright hue,
Splatters of joy and delight,
In the dance of me and you,
We create a world of light.

Brush strokes of memories made,
In joyous strokes, we embrace,
In this art, love won't fade,
A masterpiece time can't erase.

Together, we'll sketch and play,
With every giggle and cheer,
As the light fades into gray,
Our laughter will draw us near.

A canvas where hearts collide,
With each laugh, we're intertwined,
In the gallery of our pride,
A love like this, so well-defined.

Chasing Shadows Together

Beneath the twilight's soft glow,
We chase the whispers of night,
With hands held tight, we both go,
Finding paths in fading light.

Through trees where shadows dance,
We hear the quiet call of dark,
Every step a mystic chance,
In the stillness, we leave our mark.

With laughter ringing like bells,
We weave dreams into the dusk,
Exploring where the magic dwells,
In the air, both sweet and husk.

As stars begin to appear,
We share secrets, soft and low,
In the warmth, there's nothing to fear,
Together, through shadows we flow.

In the night, we close our eyes,
Chasing sunsets, letting go,
With you, my spirit flies,
In this dance of shadows, we grow.

Whispers Under the Stars

In the night sky, dreams take flight,
Stars twinkle softly, a guiding light.
Whispers dance on the gentle breeze,
Carrying hopes through the swaying trees.

Each secret shared in moonlit glow,
Bound by the magic that we both know.
The universe listens, holds us near,
In this serene moment, there's nothing to fear.

Together we wander, hearts intertwined,
Wrapped in the peace that we both find.
The night's embrace cradles our souls,
As we share our dreams, each one unfolds.

In silence we laugh, in silence we sigh,
Under the starlit canvas, you and I.
With every whisper, the cosmos sings,
A symphony born from the love that it brings.

The Garden of Companionship

In the garden where friendship grows,
Beneath the sun, our laughter flows.
Petals of trust in fragrant air,
Together we tend, with utmost care.

Each flower blooms with stories shared,
Moments cherished, a bond declared.
Roots entwined in the soil of time,
Our hearts entwined, a perfect rhyme.

Through seasons change, through sun and rain,
We nurture dreams, dismiss the pain.
In each bloom, a memory shines,
A tapestry woven in loving lines.

As twilight falls, the garden glows,
With whispered secrets only we know.
In the silence, love's beauty shows,
In the garden of companionship, it flows.

Together in the Silence

In the hush of night, we find our place,
Two souls at peace, a gentle embrace.
Words unspoken fill the air,
A quiet understanding, beyond compare.

The world outside fades to a blur,
In this moment, it's just us, for sure.
With every heartbeat, time stands still,
In silence, we listen to love's sweet thrill.

Stars twinkle softly, our silent guide,
Hand in hand, we take this ride.
No need for chatter, no need for haste,
In the silence, we find our space.

A symphony composed without a sound,
In the stillness, our souls are found.
Together we linger, in tranquil bliss,
In silence, we revel in love's pure kiss.

Echoes of Unspoken Trust

In the quiet moments, trust takes flight,
Unseen connections, a bond so tight.
Heartbeats echo, a rhythm understood,
In this sacred space, we both feel good.

Words may falter, but feelings remain,
In the silence, we share the pain.
With every glance, unspoken tales,
In the journey together, love prevails.

The whispers of trust, like shadows cast,
In each heartbeat, the spell is vast.
Through every storm and every test,
We find in each other, our perfect rest.

In the tapestry of life, threads intertwine,
Creating a picture of love so divine.
In echoes of silence, we have found,
A boundless trust that knows no bound.

A Tapestry of Kindred Spirits

In the weaving of our days,
Threads of laughter and of tears,
Each moment, rich with meaning,
A tapestry of shared years.

Hand in hand through shadows cast,
We gather joy from every part,
In the fabric of our lives,
Together we create our art.

Every story softly told,
Stitched with kindness, never frayed,
A legacy of love's embrace,
In every hue, our souls displayed.

Bound by dreams that intertwine,
Colors bright and shadows deep,
In every pattern we can find,
The joy of promises we keep.

Through time's hands, we will remain,
As kindred spirits, ever near,
In this beautiful expanse,
Our hearts will always gather here.

Rays of Shared Joy

Like sunlight through the trees,
Our laughter fills the air,
Moments spark like fireflies,
Together, we are rare.

In every smile we share,
Shadows fade away,
As warmth surrounds our hearts,
Brightening the day.

Through trials and through triumphs,
We lift each other high,
United in our purpose,
Together, we can fly.

With open hearts, we gather,
Like blossoms in the spring,
In every ray of kindness,
A sweet symphony we sing.

In life's dance of joy,
May we forever stay,
Hand in hand, heart to heart,
Creating our own way.

The Dance of Shared Dreams

In the twilight's gentle glow,
We waltz beneath the stars,
In every step we take,
Our journey feels like ours.

Dreams entwined, we sail,
On winds of hope and cheer,
With every whispered promise,
The path ahead is clear.

With every rise and fall,
We learn the steps anew,
As rhythms shift and flow,
Our spirits dance in hue.

Each twirl a celebration,
Of hopes we hold so dear,
In this dance of dreams,
We find our hearts sincere.

Through every beat and turn,
Together we will stand,
In the dance of shared dreams,
A partner's heart in hand.

Journeys Side by Side

On winding paths, we wander,
With voices soft and clear,
With every step together,
We conquer doubt and fear.

Side by side in the sunshine,
Through storms and gentle rain,
In every twist and turn,
We find our strength again.

With maps drawn in our laughter,
And love that lights the way,
Each journey that we cherish,
Becomes a part of play.

As seasons shift and alter,
Our bond will only grow,
In each adventure taken,
There's warmth we both can know.

In this life, hand in hand,
No moment is denied,
Together we'll keep walking,
On journeys side by side.

Navigating Life's Currents

We sail on waves of hopes,
With winds that guide our way.
Through storms that twist and turn,
We find the light of day.

Each ripple tells a story,
Of laughter, love, and pain.
The sea may change its course,
But dreams will still remain.

In harbors, bonds are formed,
With anchors holding tight.
We learn to dance with tides,
While reaching for the light.

So let us chart our course,
With stars to lead us home.
In currents deep and wide,
Together we will roam.

With every ebb and flow,
Our spirits intertwine.
Navigating life's paths,
In harmony, we shine.

Seeds of Trust Sprouting

In the garden of our hearts,
Seeds of trust are sown with care.
With patience, love, and warmth,
They flourish in the air.

Sprouting gently in the sun,
Roots entwined beneath the ground.
Through storms, our faith will grow,
In bonds forever found.

Each moment, we nurture light,
Watering dreams each day.
Together, hand in hand,
We weave a brighter way.

Blossoms bloom with colors bright,
Fragrance fills the air.
In this space of growth and peace,
We find what we can share.

With time our garden thrives,
A tapestry of trust.
From fragile seeds to trees,
In love, we place our trust.

A Journey Mapped in Hearts

With footprints side by side,
Our journey unfolds anew.
Two paths converge as one,
With every step, we grew.

Maps etched in laughter's lines,
And in whispers soft and true.
Through mountains and valleys,
Together, we pursue.

Every heartbeat marks a trail,
Every glance writes a page.
In this book of shared moments,
Love is our true sage.

Through shadows and through light,
We chart what lies ahead.
A journey filled with dreams,
In faith, we walk instead.

With passion as our guide,
And trust to light the way,
A journey mapped in hearts,
Will lead us home to stay.

The Embrace of Luminous Souls

In the twilight's gentle glow,
Luminous souls intertwine.
Through laughter's vibrant threads,
We find a love divine.

With open hearts we gather,
To share each joy and woe.
In the silence of the night,
Our spirits start to flow.

Embracing every shadow,
We dance beneath the stars.
Together, bright and hopeful,
No burden feels like ours.

In whispers of the moonlight,
Connection we will weave.
With every shared moment,
Our hearts shall dare to believe.

For in the warmth of closeness,
Together we will thrive.
In the embrace of luminous souls,
We find a way to rise.

Reflections of Affection

In quiet moments, hearts align,
Soft whispers dance, so sweet, divine.
A glance exchanged, love's gentle grace,
In every look, a warm embrace.

Memories weave through time's embrace,
Golden threads in a tender space.
Through laughter shared and silent tears,
Love's resonance, across the years.

Each touch ignites a spark so bright,
Guiding souls through darkest night.
Beneath the stars, where dreams take flight,
In love's soft glow, all feels right.

Amidst the chaos, peace we find,
Two souls entwined, forever kind.
In quiet corners, hearts will sigh,
Reflections of love, reaching high.

So let us treasure every day,
In love's embrace, we find our way.
Through ebb and flow, we boldly steer,
In reflections, our hearts are clear.

Uncharted Paths

Through forests dense, where shadows play,
We wander forth, come what may.
With hearts ablaze, we chase the dawn,
In uncharted paths, we carry on.

Each twist and turn unveils a dream,
With every step, we seek the theme.
The unknown calls, a siren's song,
In wild terrain, we can't go wrong.

Beneath the stars, we share our fears,
With whispered hopes and shared cheers.
Together, strong, we break the mold,
In courage found, our dreams unfold.

Through mountains high and rivers wide,
Side by side, we will abide.
With courage fierce, hearts intertwined,
In uncharted paths, our fates aligned.

So here we stand, brave and free,
In every challenge, we will see.
With open hearts, we seek the start,
Uncharted paths lead us to art.

The Comfort of Familiarity

In gentle sighs, we find our way,
Through everyday, both bright and gray.
The scent of home, a warm embrace,
In simple joys, we find our place.

Familiar tunes, they wrap around,
In every note, love's echo found.
With laughter shared, and stories told,
The comfort in the days of old.

The worn-out chair, the cozy nook,
In every corner, a cherished book.
Where time stands still, our spirits soar,
In familiarity, we seek for more.

Through trials faced, hand in hand,
Together strong, we understand.
A bond that grows in tender light,
In familiar arms, we feel so right.

So let us cherish all we know,
Through highs and lows, together grow.
In comfort found, our hearts will sing,
The joy in familiarity we bring.

Wings of Support

In times of need, you take my hand,
With gentle strength, we understand.
Your wings unfold, a sheltering grace,
In every trial, love's warm embrace.

Through stormy nights and skies so bleak,
Your voice a light, when words feel weak.
With steadfast hearts that never sway,
Together we find a better way.

In laughter shared and tears that fall,
With you beside, I stand up tall.
Your faith in me, like sunlight bright,
Guides me home, through darkest night.

As rivers flow, our love will grow,
In every challenge, strength we show.
With wings of trust, we rise and soar,
On paths we carve, forevermore.

So here we stand, proud and free,
In the dance of support, you and me.
With hearts aligned, we'll reach the skies,
In wings of support, our spirits rise.

Lanterns of Mutual Light

In the quiet night sky, they glow,
Whispers of kindness softly flow.
Each lantern shines with a story bright,
Guiding us home with shared light.

Hands held tight under the stars,
No distance feels too far,
With every flicker, hopes ignite,
Together we rise, hearts taking flight.

Echoes of laughter dance in air,
Bonds of love that we all share.
These lanterns float, dreams in sway,
Illuminating each lovely way.

Through the dark, they lead us on,
With every dusk, a brand-new dawn.
For in this glow, we find our place,
A tapestry of light and grace.

A Soulful Gathering

In a circle of dreams, we unite,
Voices blending, hearts take flight.
Around the fire, spirits soar,
In this moment, we are more.

Tales unfold, wisdom we share,
Laughter echoes, released in air.
Each glance tells a story untold,
In this warmth, we feel bold.

Words weave softly like a song,
Reminding us where we belong.
In our embrace, the world feels right,
Together we glow, pure delight.

Connections deep as ocean's blue,
In quiet strength, we find what's true.
With every heartbeat, we create,
A soulful bond that transcends fate.

Weaving Together Destiny

Threads of fate in colors bright,
Weaving dreams, a shared delight.
With every stitch, our lives entwine,
Creating stories, yours and mine.

In the loom of time, we draw near,
Crafting moments, holding dear.
With every knot, we bind our hearts,
A masterpiece where love imparts.

Patterns form through tears and cheers,
Woven with laughter, hopes, and fears.
Together we shape our journey's goal,
In this tapestry, we find our soul.

As threads converge, we find our way,
Brighter colors lead the day.
In unity, our paths connect,
A woven fate, we all reflect.

Friendship's Silent Melody

In whispers soft, our hearts take flight,
A melody sung in the quiet night.
Each note a bond that time won't sever,
In silent strength, we stand together.

Through laughter shared and tears we shed,
This silent song fills every thread.
A symphony where souls align,
Friendship's tune, a sacred sign.

In moments still, we know the tune,
A harmony beneath the moon.
Every heartbeat sings the same,
An endless song, a sweet refrain.

Across the years, through joy and strife,
This melody colors our life.
Together we dance, our spirits free,
In friendship's song, we simply be.

Luminescence of Togetherness

In the glow of a shared light,
Hands intertwined, hearts bright.
Every laugh a spark we weave,
In this dream, we believe.

Through the shadows, we stand tall,
Echoes of joy will never fall.
Together, we chase the dawn,
In the warmth, fear is gone.

From whispers to shouts we sing,
Love's melody, the joy we bring.
With each step, our souls unite,
A radiant bond, pure delight.

Through the storms, we find our way,
Countless stars guide our play.
Together, we'll always thrive,
In this light, we come alive.

Starlit Pathways Together

Beneath the canvas of the night,
We wander, hearts taking flight.
Stars like lanterns in our eyes,
Reflecting dreams that touch the skies.

Each step whispers secrets true,
In the dark, I walk with you.
Together, we weave our way,
Turning night into a day.

The moonlight dances on our skin,
Guiding moments deep within.
In your smile, I find the spark,
Leading us through the stark.

With every breath, we share a tale,
Navigating love's soft trail.
Hand in hand, our spirits soar,
Together, we forevermore.

Whispers of Our Stories

In the hush of twilight's peace,
Our tales blend, never to cease.
Echoes of laughter fill the air,
Moments shared, beyond compare.

From whispered dreams to heartfelt sighs,
Each word a treasure, love defies.
Through trials faced and journeys crossed,
In every loss, we find what's lost.

With the sun's kiss, our memories glow,
Holding close what we both know.
Stories written in the stars,
Binding souls despite the scars.

As pages turn and time moves on,
Our memories linger, never gone.
In the book of us, words align,
Whispers echo, forever shine.

The Quilt of Us

Stitched together, pieces bright,
Fabric woven, warmth and light.
In every seam, our laughter hums,
Together, love's sweet music drums.

Threads of joy and moments shared,
Hand in hand, show we cared.
Each patch tells a tale divine,
In this quilt, your heart is mine.

Colors fade but never part,
Warm embrace, a work of heart.
Through the storms, we find our way,
In this canvas, love will stay.

With every stitch, a bond we weave,
In this warmth, we can believe.
The quilt of us, forever true,
In every thread, I find you.

The Calm in Chaotic Waters

In storms that rage and howl at night,
We find our peace, a gentle light.
Through waves that crash and skies of gray,
Our hearts will guide, won't drift away.

Together we stand, side by side,
Facing the tides, a faithful ride.
No tempest can shake this bond so strong,
In chaos, together, we will belong.

Each splash of fear, we hold and tame,
With whispered hopes, we fuel the flame.
In swirling depths, our trust will grow,
As currents shift, we ebb and flow.

An anchor in the wildest sea,
Your hand in mine, we're meant to be.
When waters churn and dark clouds loom,
We'll build our shelter, love will bloom.

So let the storms come crashing down,
We'll wear our courage like a crown.
The calm will rise, we shall embrace,
In chaotic waters, we find our place.

The Lighthouse of Togetherness

In the harbor where dreams align,
You are the beacon, forever shine.
With every storm that we survive,
Your light guides me, I feel alive.

Through fog and fear, you show the way,
In darkest nights, we find our day.
Together, we weather every tide,
With you, my love, I take the ride.

A lighthouse tall, our hearts entwined,
Your warmth, my safe, my peace of mind.
Each wave that crashes, we stand tall,
In unity's strength, we'll never fall.

As ships may falter, drift and roam,
In your embrace, I find my home.
The light you give dispels the gloom,
Together we'll rise, forever bloom.

So here's to us, our guiding star,
No distance great, no journey far.
With love's fierce light, we'll always see,
In togetherness, we're truly free.

Tidal Waves of Affection

With every tide that kisses shore,
I feel your love, it's there and more.
You are the ocean, deep and wide,
In tidal waves, I want to ride.

Our hearts collide like crashing waves,
Each surge of feeling, bold and brave.
With every rush, we learn to trust,
In love's embrace, it's more than lust.

The rhythm holds a soothing sway,
In salty breezes, we'll drift away.
With every swell, my soul ignites,
In ocean's depths, we find new heights.

Together we dance on sandy shores,
With laughter bright, our spirit soars.
Through tranquil nights and sunny days,
What matters most are love's true ways.

So let the tides forever change,
Our hearts will find what feels so strange.
In tidal waves, we'll never part,
In every swell, you hold my heart.

A Symphony Unfolds

In quiet halls where music flows,
A symphony of life bestows.
With notes that lift and chords that sway,
In melodies, we find our way.

Each heartbeat plays a gentle tune,
Under the glow of a silver moon.
We dance through rhythms, hand in hand,
In perfect harmony, we stand.

The strings, they weave a tapestry,
Of love and laughter, wild and free.
With every sound, our spirits climb,
In unity, we conquer time.

As crescendos rise and echoes fall,
We blend our dreams, we give our all.
The symphony, it tells our tale,
In every note, we shall prevail.

So let the music fill the air,
In every sound, your essence there.
Together, love, we boldly mold,
A symphony within unfolds.

Journeys Hand in Hand

Through winding paths we take our stand,
With every step, we walk hand in hand.
The sun will rise, the stars will glow,
In unity, our spirits flow.

From mountain high to valley low,
We share our dreams, watch them grow.
With laughter shared and whispers light,
In this journey, hearts ignite.

The road may twist, the weather change,
Yet with each other, we feel no strange.
Together we face what life just sends,
In every twist, our love transcends.

Through the storms and shining days,
Our bond deepens in countless ways.
With every challenge, hand in hand,
We carve our names in shifting sand.

So here's to journeys, far and wide,
Together forever, our hearts are tied.
In every moment, let it be known,
With you beside me, I am home.

A Symphony of Kindred Spirits

In harmony, we sing our song,
With melodies that pull us along.
Each note a whisper of our hearts,
In symphony, the magic starts.

Together in the dance of fate,
We celebrate and resonate.
With every rhythm, sacred trust,
In unity, our spirits gust.

Through highs and lows, we find the beat,
In every pause, our souls meet.
With laughter bright and tears that blend,
This symphony, we shall defend.

As seasons change and time does flow,
Our bond grows deep, yet light as snow.
In every chorus, strong and free,
Kindred spirits, you and me.

So let the music fill the air,
With notes of love beyond compare.
In this sweet song, we find our way,
A timeless dance, come what may.

The Colors of Companionship

In vibrant hues, our lives entwine,
With every shade, our hearts align.
From dawn's soft blush to dusk's deep blue,
In colors bright, I see you true.

Together we paint the world anew,
With strokes of laughter, with dreams in view.
Each moment cherished, bright and bold,
In shades of friendship, love unfolds.

Through stormy skies and sunny days,
Our palette shifts in countless ways.
With every brush, a story told,
In colors of warmth, we break the cold.

With every hue, our spirits soar,
In every tone, we ask for more.
The canvas wide, the hearts entwined,
In every color, love we find.

So here's to the shades that we explore,
In vibrant friendship, forevermore.
Together we'll paint, with brush in hand,
A masterpiece across the land.

Unseen Ties

In shadows cast, our spirits bind,
Through unseen threads, our hearts aligned.
A whisper soft, a gentle sigh,
In silent moments, we learn to fly.

Though distance stretches, it cannot break,
The bond we hold for friendship's sake.
Invisible strings pull us near,
In every heartbeat, I feel you here.

Behind the laughter, beneath the tears,
The ties run deep, transcending years.
In quiet moments, we share the weight,
Of life's great gifts and the heavy fate.

With unspoken words, we understand,
The beauty found in a gentle hand.
In every glance, in every pause,
These unseen ties hold no cause.

So here's to bonds that time can't sever,
In heartbeats shared, we're strong together.
In life's great tapestry, we find,
These unseen ties that love designed.

The Nature of Togetherness

In the garden where we grow,
Roots entwined, a gentle flow.
Sunshine pours, and shadows play,
In each moment, we will stay.

With each breath, our spirits blend,
A melody, on love depends.
In laughter's echo, faith will soar,
Together here, we seek no more.

Through the waves of dusk and dawn,
Hand in hand, we carry on.
Every challenge, we defy,
Tied by bonds that never die.

In the silence, find our trust,
In the heart, it's surely just.
Nature speaks in whispers sweet,
Together, makes our lives complete.

From the roots to skies above,
We plant seeds with endless love.
In our journey, flowers bloom,
In togetherness, there's room.

Holding Hands Through Storms

When the thunder shakes the night,
I will hold your hand so tight.
Through the tempest, we will stand,
Braving together, heart to hand.

As the rain begins to fall,
In your strength, I find it all.
Every struggle that we face,
With your touch, I find my place.

Lightning strikes, but we won't break,
Stormy seas cannot forsake.
In the eye, a moment's calm,
With your warmth, I feel the balm.

Through the darkest clouds we steer,
With your voice, I have no fear.
Side by side, we face the night,
In each heartbeat, there's the light.

When the sun breaks through the gray,
We will dance the storms away.
Hand in hand, we rise once more,
Stronger still, our spirits soar.

Our Hearts' Gentle Whisper

In the quiet of the night,
Hearts convene, a soft delight.
Whispers linger, dreams unfold,
Stories of love, gently told.

In the gaze, a secret shared,
In your eyes, I find you bared.
With each heartbeat, truths ignite,
In our souls, we take to flight.

Through the whispers, soft as air,
In your presence, none compare.
Moments paused in still embrace,
In this silence, we find grace.

While the world spins loud and fast,
In your heart, I feel my past.
Every sigh and tender glance,
In our music, life's sweet dance.

As we journey hand in hand,
In the whisper, we will stand.
Hearts entwined, a story true,
Every whisper leads to you.

Reflections of Each Other

In the mirror, your face I see,
Every glance reflects the key.
Together, shaping who we are,
In our eyes, we find the star.

Through the laughter and the tears,
You are part of all my years.
Every moment, shared with grace,
In our paths, we leave a trace.

In each trial we've overcome,
Two as one, we hear the drum.
Every step, a dance of trust,
In our souls, a bond that's just.

Like the sun and moon above,
We're reflections, pure with love.
In the shadows, light will glow,
With our hearts, the truth will flow.

As we journey, hand in hand,
In your heart, I understand.
Reflections in the dark and light,
Together, we will shine so bright.

Bonds Beyond Time

In the silence of the night,
Stars whisper ancient tales,
Of friendships forged in fire,
As time gently unveils.

Moments captured in a frame,
Memories woven tight,
Through laughter and through pain,
Our spirits take to flight.

Seasons change, yet we remain,
Like trees that bend but stand,
Rooted deep in love's embrace,
In this ever-changing land.

Time may pass, the world may shift,
Yet hearts still beat as one,
With every trial, every gift,
We rise beneath the sun.

A tapestry of joy and tears,
Threads of fate intertwined,
In the fabric of our years,
Eternally aligned.

Echoes of Shared Laughter

In the corners of our minds,
Laughter lingers soft and sweet,
Like echoes of the past,
Where joy and heartbeats meet.

Every joke, a cherished gem,
Shared with glances, fleeting smiles,
They weave a bond so profound,
Spanning miles and endless miles.

Whispers in the evening air,
Warming souls, igniting light,
Reminders that we've journeyed far,
Through shadows into bright.

Even in the darkest days,
Laughter finds a way to bloom,
A melody that lifts us high,
Dispelling all the gloom.

In the dance of shared delight,
We find our common ground,
Echoes of our laughter strong,
In every joy unbound.

In the Garden of Togetherness

In a garden lush and green,
Seeds of love are gently sown,
Amongst the blooms of kindness,
Together, we have grown.

Hand in hand, we tend the soil,
Nurturing what's meant to thrive,
Each petal holds a story,
Where memories come alive.

Raindrops fall, a sweet caress,
Sunlight dances through the leaves,
With every season's gentle change,
A deeper bond achieves.

Among the vines and fragrant herbs,
We find our hearts entwined,
In the whispers of the breeze,
Love's promise redefined.

In the garden of our dreams,
Together we will stand,
With every flower's bloom,
We nurture love's demand.

Threads of Connection

Each thread, a story intertwined,
Binding us in colors bright,
With laughter, tears, and joy,
We weave through day and night.

In the fabric of our lives,
Stitches made with care and grace,
Each moment, every smile,
Leaves an imprint in this space.

Though the world may pull apart,
Like fibers strained and worn,
Our connections hold us strong,
In love, we are reborn.

With gentle hands, we mend and patch,
Embracing every flaw,
In the masterpiece we make,
There lies a sacred law.

As seasons fade and change takes hold,
The threads remain so true,
In the tapestry of souls,
I am forever bound to you.

Interwoven Dreams

In twilight's glow, we weave our dreams,
Threads of hope and gentle schemes.
With whispered words, our hearts align,
In a tapestry where stars entwine.

Underneath the silver sky,
We share our fears, we let out sighs.
Together we rise, together we fall,
In this dance, we give our all.

Each step we take is hand in hand,
Building castles in the sand.
The tides will come, the winds may change,
Yet our dreams will never rearrange.

In silence deep, our souls connect,
With every smile, we reflect.
A bond so strong, it knows no end,
In this journey, we transcend.

So here's to dreams that never fade,
A masterpiece that we've portrayed.
In every heartbeat, every sigh,
Together, we will always fly.

A Haven of Shared Hope

In a quiet space where tales unfold,
A haven bright, a heart of gold.
Where laughter streams and sorrows cease,
In shared hopes, we find our peace.

With every dawn, we greet the light,
A promise made, hearts taking flight.
In gentle whispers, dreams ignite,
Guiding us through the longest night.

In every moment that we share,
A piece of love is in the air.
In every glance, a spark will glow,
A haven where our spirits grow.

Through storms that come, we stand as one,
A bond so fierce, it can't be undone.
In unity, our voices sing,
A haven shared, true hope we bring.

So hand in hand, let's shape our fate,
In this haven, we celebrate.
With hearts wide open, dreams will bloom,
In shared hope, we cast away gloom.

Dreams That Dance Together

In moonlit nights, our dreams take flight,
They twirl and leap in pure delight.
With every rhythm, our hearts collide,
In this grand dance, we both confide.

Each heartbeat echoes, soft and sweet,
A melody that feels complete.
In laughter's tune, we lose our cares,
With dreams that soar, our souls declare.

As stars align in skies above,
We sway together, wrapped in love.
Through highs and lows, we'll always dance,
In every step, we find our chance.

With every glance, our spirits sing,
In this duet, joy we bring.
Together we weave a story bright,
Of dreams that dance, swimming in light.

So take my hand, let's chase the dawn,
With dreams that dance, we carry on.
In unity, our hearts will sway,
In this beautiful ballet, we'll stay.

The Spirit of Companionship

In the quiet hum of a shared day,
The spirit of companionship leads the way.
Through laughter shared and tears that fall,
Together, we can conquer all.

With open hearts and eager minds,
In every story, a truth finds.
Through every trial, we stand as one,
In the warmth of friendship, life's never done.

In moments bright and shadows deep,
The spirit of trust is ours to keep.
With shoulders strong and hands held tight,
We face the dark, embracing the light.

Through ages past and days to come,
In every heartbeat, we have succumbed.
With bonds so rich and spirits free,
In companionship, we find our glee.

So here's to us, in all we share,
The spirit of camaraderie, beyond compare.
With every breath, let's cherish this gift,
In the spirit of companionship, we uplift.

Shadows That Dance in Light

Beneath the trees, shadows play,
Whispers of dreams, the night turns to day.
Fleeting glimpses, soft and bright,
In every corner, dance the light.

A gentle breeze stirs the air,
Caressing moments, free from care.
Like fleeting thoughts that dare to roam,
In the warmth of light, we find our home.

Colors blend in twinkling hues,
Nature's patterns, a timeless muse.
Shadows whisper secrets old,
In their dance, our stories unfold.

The moon drapes silver on the ground,
Echoes of laughter softly resound.
In every flicker, hope takes flight,
Shadows that dance in the heart of night.

With every pulse, the world takes wing,
A symphony of life, we sing.
Beneath the stars, we find our place,
In shadows bright, we embrace grace.

A Journey of Hopeful Hearts

Across the valleys, dreams take flight,
Guided by stars, through the endless night.
With every step, we seek the sun,
A journey begun, together as one.

Hand in hand, we rise and shine,
In every struggle, our spirits align.
With laughter and tears, we pave the way,
Hope blooms golden, come what may.

Mountains high, rivers run deep,
In the heart's cradle, promises keep.
Through the tempest, our voices soar,
Hopeful hearts, forever explore.

Each sunrise whispers, "Don't despair,"
In the face of trials, courage we share.
Together we dream, together we start,
On this journey, hope's our heart.

In every moment, joy is found,
With every heartbeat, love's profound.
Through valleys low, and peaks so bright,
We write our tale, hopeful hearts ignite.

The Echo of Shared Laughter

In the garden where joy aligns,
Laughter bubbles like sparkling wines.
A melody shared, it fills the air,
Moments woven, beyond compare.

With every chuckle, shadows fade,
In the warmth of smiles, love is laid.
Echoes dancing, side by side,
In the heart's rhythm, we take pride.

Time stands still with friends so dear,
In the sound of laughter, we shed fear.
Stories brighten the darkest night,
Shared laughter, our guiding light.

Through the seasons, hand in hand,
Life's small treasures, we understand.
In echoes of joy, our spirits climb,
Together we flourish, bated time.

In each ripple of joyous sound,
A tapestry of love is found.
As laughter lingers, hearts unite,
An echo remains, pure and bright.

A Voyage Rooted in Care

With sails unfurled, we chart our course,
Through waves of life, we feel its force.
In every heartbeat, a guiding star,
A voyage begins, no matter how far.

Together we navigate the storm,
In the face of tempests, we keep warm.
With hands that steady and eyes that share,
This journey is crafted with tender care.

Mountains loom, and oceans wide,
With love as our anchor, we shall abide.
In every challenge, our spirits rise,
Rooted in care, beneath vast skies.

Every port holds tales anew,
Adventures blossom, in shades of blue.
Through laughter and trials, we set our sail,
A voyage of hearts shall never fail.

In the waters deep, bonds we create,
Together we journey, it's never too late.
With faith as our compass, we boldly steer,
In this voyage of care, we forge our sphere.

In the Heart of Companionship

In laughter shared and whispered dreams,
We carve a space where sunlight beams.
Through trials faced, we rise anew,
Each moment deep, just me and you.

With hands entwined, we walk the road,
In simple joys, our hearts explode.
Every smile and every tear,
Brings us closer, year by year.

Together we have built a nest,
In storms, we find our strength, our rest.
A bond unbreakable, firm and true,
In the heart of companionship, just me and you.

Memories like stars, they shine so bright,
Guiding us through the darkest night.
With every heartbeat, love will grow,
In this embrace, we both will know.

In quiet moments, silence speaks,
The language of love, it softly peaks.
In the heart of companionship,
Forevermore, our souls shall grip.

United Under the Moonlight

Beneath the sky where shadows weave,
We find our dreams, we dare believe.
The stars above, a timeless dance,
In the moonlight's glow, we take our chance.

With every glance, a story told,
Of warmth in winter, of hearts bold.
A gentle breeze whispers sweetly near,
Together we chase away the fear.

United under the moon's embrace,
We share our wishes, our sacred space.
In every sigh, our spirits blend,
A journey found, where hearts transcend.

As clouds drift by, the world feels new,
In this moment, it's just us two.
The silver light reflects our dreams,
In the night's heart, we are supreme.

With hands held tight, we watch the tide,
In the moonlit glow, there's nothing to hide.
United forever, side by side,
In the warmth of love, we shall abide.

The Radiance of Together

In the morning light, we rise as one,
Each day anew, our journey begun.
With shared laughter and gentle care,
We light the shadows, always aware.

Through every challenge that may arise,
We find the strength to reach the skies.
In every heartbeat, a promise made,
In the radiance of together, love won't fade.

With every sunset, we pause and see,
The beauty of moments, just you and me.
In the colors that swirl, our dreams ignite,
Painting our world with joy and delight.

As seasons shift, we hold so tight,
Through rain and shine, our souls unite.
In the warmth of love, our hearts agree,
In the radiance of together, we are free.

Hand in hand, we face what's next,
A tapestry woven, life's little text.
In each embrace, our spirits soar,
In the radiance of together, we want more.

The Strength We Share

In quiet moments, we stand as one,
The battles fought, the victories won.
Through whispered words and knowing glances,
In the strength we share, true love enhances.

With every heartbeat, we lend a hand,
In this journey, together we stand.
Facing the storms that life may send,
With open hearts, we always mend.

The weight of the world, we bravely bear,
In our embrace, we find the fair.
Through every trial, through every care,
In the strength we share, love's witness fair.

In laughter loud, our spirits rise,
In moments shared, we touch the skies.
With every challenge, we rise and dare,
In the strength we share, nothing can compare.

Together we build, our dreams take flight,
In shadows dark, we find the light.
With every heartbeat, we declare,
In the strength we share, a love so rare.

Lighthouses in the Storm

Amidst the raging waves, they stand tall,
Guiding lost souls through the darkest squall.
Beacons of hope in tempest's embrace,
Shining their light with unwavering grace.

With weathered stones and a steadfast glow,
They whisper tales of the seas below.
Guardians of secrets, ancient and wise,
Watching the world with unblinking eyes.

Through lightning and thunder, they hold the line,
A promise of safety, their light divine.
Each flash tells a story of ships that bled,
Of journeys begun and the paths they tread.

So here's to the lighthouses, brave and bright,
In storms that challenge both sea and night.
A symbol of strength when the world feels torn,
Everlasting guides, forever reborn.

Paths That Converge

Two trails entwined beneath the trees,
Whispering stories carried by the breeze.
Footsteps echo where hearts once roamed,
In the dance of fate, they found their home.

Crossroads of dreams and shared delight,
Illuminated paths by morning light.
With each step forward, they intertwine,
Creating a tapestry, unique and divine.

Laughter and tears, the journey they trace,
Moments of stillness, a warm embrace.
In every twist and turn, they find a way,
Guided by love, come what may.

As seasons change and footprints fade,
The bonds of friendship will never jade.
For in the heart's compass, they shall abide,
The paths that converge, forever side by side.

The Heartbeat of Belonging

In the quiet corners of each space,
Lives the gentle pulse of a warm embrace.
Ties that bind in laughter and tears,
Whispers of comfort chasing away fears.

Shared moments linger like sweet perfume,
Filling the air in a crowded room.
Invisible threads weave stories untold,
A tapestry rich, both tender and bold.

Through storms and sun, the rhythm persists,
An orchestra playing through life's twists.
Hands held together, hearts deeply sung,
In the dance of belonging, we all belong.

Echoes of laughter, voices ethereal,
In the heartbeat of belonging, we feel surreal.
Though distance may call, and time may demand,
We're anchored together, forever hand in hand.

Timeless Treasures

Hidden in shadows where memories dwell,
Are treasures that time will never quell.
Photographs faded, yet visions so clear,
Echoes of laughter when loved ones draw near.

Trinkets of joy, dusted with care,
Stories encased in the soft evening air.
Each item a portal to moments sublime,
Whispers of history, echoes of time.

The old rocking chair, a haven of dreams,
Where echoes of childhood flow like streams.
Glimmers of gold in the depths of the soul,
Infusing our lives, making us whole.

A treasure is found in the heart's embrace,
In words unspoken, in love's gentle grace.
For in every heartbeat, a story is spun,
Timeless treasures cherished, never outdone.

Secrets Under the Moon

Whispers float in silver light,
Promises held through the night.
Stars above, they keep the tune,
Lost in tales under the moon.

Shadows dance on whispered dreams,
Secrets wrapped in silent schemes.
Hearts entwined in this soft glow,
Under stars, the world feels slow.

Night unfolds a sacred time,
With each breath, a silent rhyme.
Crickets sing their mellow song,
In this place, we both belong.

The moonbeam casts its gentle grace,
Lights the path of our embrace.
In the dark, our truths are laid,
In this glow, we are not afraid.

With each secret shared at night,
We find solace in the light.
Hand in hand, as shadows blend,
Under the moon, love we send.

The Bridge of True Connection

In the distance, we see it rise,
A bridge built from hope and ties.
Crossing over, hearts align,
In this space, love's design.

Every step, a journey shared,
Understanding flows, unprepared.
Words unspoken fill the air,
In silence, we show we care.

Waves below whisper our name,
Two souls dancing, avoiding blame.
Together strong, we walk the thread,
Hand in hand, fear's spread.

Moments blend in this embrace,
As we find our sacred place.
Trust sealed with every glance,
In your eyes, I see my chance.

The bridge connects our dreams at night,
Illuminated by shared light.
A bond so deep, it will not fade,
Over this bridge, love's serenade.

A Canvas of Memories

Brushstrokes of laughter in the air,
Colors dance without a care.
Moments captured, vivid, bright,
On this canvas, pure delight.

Each memory a vibrant hue,
Painted with love, tried and true.
Shadows fall, yet warmth remains,
In every joy, sweet refrains.

Layers thick with tales to tell,
In this space, we know it well.
Strokes of time, so beautifully,
Making art of you and me.

Splashes of dreams in every scene,
Framed together, a life serene.
With each stroke, our story flows,
In vibrant shades, it ever grows.

As we gaze on this masterpiece,
Every glance brings heart's release.
In this art, we live and sigh,
A canvas of memories, you and I.

The Warmth of Their Presence

In the room, a glowing light,
Soft and warm, it feels so right.
Laughter mingles, fills the air,
Each moment cherished, rare.

Like a blanket on the cold,
Their presence, a story told.
With each glance, love's embrace,
In their warmth, we find our place.

Echoes of joy, whispers sweet,
Every heartbeat, a gentle beat.
Fingers entwined, we stand so near,
In the warmth, we shed all fear.

The hours pass, but time feels still,
In their presence, hearts do fill.
Shared glances, gentle sighs,
In this warmth, the world complies.

When we part, the glow remains,
In our hearts, their love sustains.
A warmth that lingers, never dies,
In their presence, true love lies.

Embracing the Moments

In the fleeting glow of dusk,
We find the silent echoes,
Whispers of a time long past,
Moments held like precious stones.

Laughter dances on the breeze,
Softly brushing against the skin,
Each heartbeat a melody,
Played in the symphony of life.

Threads of joy woven tight,
In the fabric of our days,
Each embrace a gentle sigh,
A tapestry of love we weave.

Underneath the starlit sky,
Memories flicker, bright and bold,
A canvas painted with our hopes,
In colors rich and stories told.

So let us hold these moments dear,
With open hearts, let us rejoice,
For every breath, a gift bestowed,
In every heartbeat, we have choice.

Navigators of Life's Ocean

Sails unfurl to greet the sun,
We set forth on endless waves,
Navigators of dreams untold,
Finding treasures in the blue.

The wind whispers secrets low,
Guiding hearts to distant shores,
Casting away our silent fears,
With every swell, we learn to soar.

Stars above, our guiding lights,
In the vastness, we are one,
Together charting paths unknown,
With courage sewn into our sails.

Tides may rise and storms may roar,
Yet trust in us will not fade,
For in our hearts, we hold the map,
Of the journey that we've made.

Every wave a lesson learned,
Each ripple in the sea our guide,
We sail on, strong and unbowed,
Navigators of the tide.

The Colors We Create

With every brush, a story blooms,
On canvas bright, emotions flow,
Colors dance in vibrant hues,
A world crafted, rich and pure.

From whispered blues to fiery reds,
We paint our hopes, our dreams unfold,
In every stroke, a piece of us,
Creating tales that must be told.

A splash of laughter warms the hearts,
While shadows linger, soft yet deep,
In hues of life, both bright and dim,
Our palette holds what memories keep.

So let us blend with gentle hands,
These pigments of our shared delight,
For in this art, we find our voice,
In the colors, we ignite.

Together, we can shade the world,
With love's rich tones and friendship's spark,
In every hue, together stand,
The colors we create leave marks.

Voices in Unison

In the quiet of the night,
A chorus rises, soft and sweet,
Voices blend in harmonious song,
Echoes of hearts that beat as one.

Stories shared and laughter flowed,
In the cadence of the crowd,
We sing of hope, we sing of love,
In unity, we find our sound.

Each note a spark igniting dreams,
Melodies weave through open air,
With every voice, a life embraced,
Together, casting out despair.

As the sun dips low in light,
We gather close, hands intertwined,
In the symphony of friendship,
Our hearts forever are aligned.

So let our voices rise and soar,
Through valleys deep and mountains high,
In unison, we'll pave the way,
With every song, together fly.

A Chorus of Laughter

In the golden glow of daylight,
Laughter dances, pure and bright.
Joyful echoes fill the air,
Moments shared beyond compare.

With friends gathered, spirits soar,
Every chuckle opens doors.
Memories made in sweet delight,
Together, we chase the night.

Through every jest and playful tease,
We find a comfort, hearts at ease.
Laughter lingers, love's embrace,
In each smile, a sacred space.

The world grows lighter, worries fade,
In this symphony we've made.
A chorus built on trust and dreams,
Life's beauty shines in laughter's beams.

So gather close, hold on tight,
Let laughter guide us, pure delight.
In every giggle, every cheer,
A tapestry of joy is here.

The Comfort of Knowing

In stillness comes a gentle peace,
A comforting thought, love's release.
Knowing we're never alone,
In hearts, a warm, inviting home.

Through trials faced and paths we tread,
In whispered faith, hope is fed.
The shadows linger, but we shine,
Together, our spirits entwine.

Every stumble, every fall,
With each other, we stand tall.
The comfort found in shared embrace,
In knowing hearts, we find our place.

So when the night feels long and cold,
Remember warmth in stories told.
Together, stronger, hand in hand,
The comfort of knowing, we understand.

Through every doubt, in every sigh,
With gentle whispers, we'll fly high.
In each heartbeat, a promise lies,
The comfort of knowing never dies.

Crafted in Kindness

In every gesture, every word,
A seed of kindness, gently stirred.
Crafted moments, pure and bright,
Shining softly like the night.

A smile shared, a hand to hold,
Stories woven, love's pure gold.
In the quiet, we find our way,
Kindness blooms, brightens the day.

Through trials faced, we find our grace,
In each other's warm embrace.
Crafted memories, beauty's art,
A tapestry woven from the heart.

In small acts, immense we find,
A world transformed, hearts aligned.
With every kindness that we share,
A brighter world is ours to bear.

So let us mold with loving hands,
Create a life where kindness stands.
With courage, we'll continue to weave,
A story of love, for all to believe.

Gazing at Shared Horizons

Beneath the vast and open sky,
We gather close, hearts flying high.
Gazing forth at horizons wide,
With dreams and hopes by our side.

In every sunset, colors blend,
A canvas where our spirits mend.
Together, we face the unknown,
In shared journeys, love has grown.

Through mountains tall and valleys deep,
In whispered winds, our secrets keep.
Hand in hand, we wander free,
In every step, we find our glee.

As stars awaken in the night,
We share our dreams, soft and bright.
The universe sings a tune,
In every heart, a hopeful rune.

So let us gaze, let our hearts soar,
Finding magic forevermore.
In this journey, side by side,
Gazing at horizons, our hearts abide.

The Wonder of Us

In a world of our own dreams,
Where laughter stitches the seams,
We dance to the song of time,
Two hearts in perfect rhyme.

Under stars that never fade,
We cherish every cascade,
With whispers that softly flow,
In the magic of the glow.

Through storms that test our might,
We stand together, holding tight,
United in every stormy gust,
In each other's love, we trust.

Walking paths that intertwine,
Every moment a sacred sign,
In the wonder of silent grace,
We find our cherished place.

When shadows blend with light,
We're guided by the moon's sight,
A bond that defies the night,
Forever in love's true flight.

Blooming in Each Other's Shade

In gardens where memories grow,
We nurture love with gentle glow,
Your laughter, like petals, spreads,
In the warmth where kindness treads.

With roots that delve so deep,
Together our secrets we keep,
In petals soft, our stories thrive,
In each other's shade, we strive.

The blooms reflect our shared past,
A tapestry of love that's vast,
In colors bright and textures bold,
We cradle dreams yet untold.

Even when the winds may blow,
And clouds gather, shadows throw,
We'll shelter each other's heart,
From the storms that set apart.

In every spring, new dreams will wake,
For love's sweet kiss, we pledge to take,
Blooming boldly, hand in hand,
In life's wide and wondrous land.

The Architecture of Trust

Foundations built on honest ground,
In every promise made, we're bound,
With beams of hope and love so strong,
In the silence, we belong.

The walls that rise are made of care,
A shelter built for hearts laid bare,
In every crack, a story lives,
In the trust, our spirit gives.

Windows open to the light,
With views of love, so pure and bright,
In every room, laughter echoes clear,
In the architecture, we are here.

Rooftops sheltering dreams aloft,
In every breeze, our spirits soft,
Together, we'll weather the rain,
In this home, we break the chain.

Constructing dreams on sacred ground,
In the heart's embrace, we are found,
A legacy of love that lasts,
In the architecture, shadows cast.

A Canvas Spattered with Joy

With strokes of passion, colors flow,
On this canvas, our love will grow,
Each hue a memory bold,
In the vision, dreams unfold.

Splashes bright, like laughter's sound,
In the chaos, beauty's found,
Every brushstroke, a life we weave,
In the joy, we both believe.

Swirls of laughter, shades of glee,
Creating a masterpiece, you and me,
In every splash, a moment shared,
In this artwork, love declared.

Textures of our gentle touch,
Tell stories that mean so much,
In the blend of night and day,
We find our unique way.

As the canvas reaches wide,
In the colors, we won't hide,
Together, in joy's embrace,
A masterpiece time can't erase.

In the Embrace of Understanding

In quiet moments, hearts collide,
A gentle look, no words to hide.
We share our fears, our hopes, our dreams,
In the soft glow of silent beams.

With open minds, we take a chance,
Each thought a thread, a sacred dance.
Our worlds entwined, we build the trust,
In this embrace, it's love, it's just.

Through storms that rage, we stand as one,
With every dawn, a new day's sun.
We weave our stories, hand in hand,
In the embrace of understanding.

The whispers shared, the laughter bright,
A tapestry of purest light.
In every challenge, we find our way,
Together strong, come what may.

In this space where spirits soar,
We learn to give, to love, explore.
The language of the heart, so clear,
In the embrace, we hold what's dear.

Starlit Paths of Unity

Under a sky where starlight sings,
We walk together, our hope takes wings.
Each step a promise, each glance a thread,
In unity's glow, no words unsaid.

The night unfolds with stories told,
In the warmth of friendship, hearts turn bold.
With every twinkling star above,
We chart our course filled with love.

Through shadows deep, our light remains,
In shared laughter and joyful gains.
The paths we tread, both near and far,
Are marked by dreams, our guiding star.

Together we face the cosmic tide,
With every heartbeat, side by side.
In the dance of life, we lift our gaze,
Starlit paths, a shared embrace.

As constellations weave their light,
We find our strength within the night.
In the silence, hear the truth's decree,
In unity's arms, we are free.

Voices in the Breeze

A whisper rides upon the air,
Each voice a note, a gentle prayer.
In the rustling leaves, we find our song,
A symphony where we belong.

With every breeze that stirs the trees,
Our laughter dances like the leaves.
In harmony, our spirits soar,
Voices in the breeze, forevermore.

Through valleys deep and mountains high,
Our melodies weave and intertwine.
Each word a bridge, a bond so true,
In the breath of nature, me and you.

As winds carry tales of old,
In the warmth of hearts, we are consoled.
Together we rise, together we sing,
With voices raised, a vibrant spring.

In every moment, we are known,
In the whispering leaves, we have grown.
Through life's great journey, we all seize,
The beauty found in voices in the breeze.

Footprints on the Sand

Along the shore, where waves caress,
We leave our marks, a soft impress.
Each footprint tells a tale of love,
In the dance of tides, a gift from above.

With every step, the memories fade,
Yet in the heart, they're never traded.
Together we walk, in sun and storm,
In footprints traced, our spirits warm.

As tides erase what once stood fast,
We cherish the moments, forever cast.
In laughter's echo, we find our way,
On sandy paths where we choose to stay.

With grains of time slipping through our hands,
We savor the journey across these lands.
In every stride, a promise stays,
Footprints on the sand, through all our days.

Though waves may rise and waters churn,
In every heartbeat, we relate, we learn.
As life unfolds, together we strand,
With love in our steps, and footprints on the sand.

The Light in Each Other's Eyes

In the quiet glow, we find our way,
A flicker of hope at the break of day.
With every glance, a spark ignites,
Illuminating dreams that take to flight.

Your laughter dances like the morning sun,
Two hearts beating, forever as one.
In your gaze, I see my truth reflected,
A bond unbroken, forever connected.

Through shadows deep, we walk as two,
In every challenge, I'll stand by you.
Hand in hand, we chase the light,
Together we shine, burning bright.

With every whisper, love's gentle song,
In this harmony, we both belong.
In the stillness, our souls embrace,
Finding solace in this sacred space.

So let us cherish this radiant glow,
In the light of love, our spirits grow.
For in each other's eyes, we find,
A universe where hearts are kind.

Whispers of the Heart

In twilight's hush, our secrets blend,
With every word, our souls transcend.
Soft whispers flow within the night,
Revealing dreams in silvery light.

Each heartbeat echoes tales untold,
In this quiet bond, we find our gold.
Through gentle sighs, our stories weave,
In whispered truths, we learn to believe.

As shadows dance, our spirits soar,
In the warmth of trust, we ask for more.
With every breath, we share a part,
An endless journey, the whispers of the heart.

Through laughter shared and tears we shed,
In every moment, love is fed.
A symphony played on fragile strings,
In the silence, hope always sings.

So listen closely, let love be your guide,
In whispers soft where dreams abide.
Together in this fleeting art,
We craft a tale, whispers of the heart.

Souls Entwined

In the tapestry of time, we weave,
Threads of laughter, love, and grief.
With every moment, our colors blend,
In every heartbeat, a timeless friend.

Across the miles, our spirits reach,
In the silence, there's so much to teach.
As morning dawns and evening falls,
In every season, love gently calls.

Through myriad dreams, we both reside,
In sacred spaces, love won't hide.
With open hearts, we explore the night,
In the depths of love, we find our light.

Holding tight as the world unfolds,
In whispers shared, our story's told.
With every challenge, we grow more aligned,
In the dance of life, our souls entwined.

So take my hand as we journey on,
In this symphony, we both belong.
Together forged in love's divine,
A bond eternal, hearts intertwined.

Moments Wrapped in Wonder

In the still of night, we gaze at stars,
Counting dreams, forgetting scars.
Each twinkle tells a secret tale,
In this magic, we shall not fail.

Through the laughter and the tears we share,
In every heartbeat, you show you care.
Moments wrapped in wonder's grace,
In every glance, a warm embrace.

As seasons shift and time does flow,
In every memory, love will grow.
With open arms, we greet the dawn,
In this journey, we will carry on.

Together under moonlit skies,
In whispers soft, love never lies.
In every pause, in every sigh,
Moments cherished, as time slips by.

So let us dance through all that's seen,
In the magic of the moments in between.
With every heartbeat, we discover,
Life's greatest treasures wrapped in wonder.

Mosaic of Memories Made

Fragments of laughter, a patchwork bright,
Colors of friendship, woven in light.
Each moment crafted, with stories to share,
A mosaic of memories, treasures laid bare.

Whispers of summer and autumn's embrace,
Capturing time, in this cherished place.
Moments like canvases, painted so true,
Each brushstroke a heartbeat, a memory renewed.

Seasons may change, but the essence will stay,
In every sweet glance, you won't fade away.
A tapestry woven from dreams held tight,
Memories dance in the warm, soft light.

Bound by our stories, we cherish the past,
The pages still turning, our shadows will last.
Together we stand, hand in hand we will roam,
In this beautiful mosaic, we've found our home.

So here's to the laughter and times spent with grace,
To the mosaic of memories, our favorite place.
Though years may keep moving, they'll always remain,
The stories we tell are the joy and the pain.

Beneath the Same Sky

Under the vastness, we gather and dream,
Stars like our hopes, they shimmer and gleam.
Connected by whispers, from valley to peak,
Beneath the same sky, it's love that we seek.

Clouds drift like thoughts, soft and serene,
Caressing the earth with a gentle sheen.
Moments are fleeting, yet time stands still,
Beneath the same sky, our hearts feel the thrill.

Daylight may wane, giving way to the night,
Yet constellations linger, shining so bright.
In silence we gather, in shadows we play,
Beneath the same sky, come what may.

Each sunrise a blessing, each sunset a sigh,
Promises whispered, as dreams soar high.
From every corner, together we rise,
Beneath the same sky, we share our goodbyes.

So let us remember, in laughter and tears,
Beneath the same sky, we conquer our fears.
Together we'll wander, through night and through day,
Bound by the love that will never decay.

Harvesting the Moments

In fields of golden, where sunflowers sway,
We gather the moments, at dusk and at day.
Each leaf tells a story, each breeze holds a sigh,
Harvesting the moments that bid time goodbye.

With hands full of joy, we gather the seeds,
Planting tomorrow, fulfilling our needs.
In laughter and whispers, our hearts intertwine,
Harvesting moments, life's love in each line.

Through seasons of change, we learn and we grow,
Each trial a lesson, each smile a glow.
In gardens of memory, together we strive,
Harvesting the moments that keep us alive.

So let us rejoice in the fruits that we share,
In fields rich with kindness, a bounty so rare.
Together we nurture, through trials we roam,
Harvesting each moment, we've made it our home.

With every sunrise, a new chance to see,
All the beauty surrounding, in you and in me.
As we plant our roots deeper, our spirits will soar,
Harvesting the moments, forever we'll adore.

Bridges of Understanding

Across the divide, our hearts reach and call,
Building the bridges that connect us all.
In silence and solace, we share and we mend,
Bridges of understanding, where differences end.

Words are our pathways, each story a thread,
Through laughter and learning, our spirits are fed.
In kindness and patience, we wander and roam,
Bridges of understanding, creating our home.

As rivers of time flow, they carve through the stone,
Bringing us closer, never alone.
In the dance of connection, our lives intertwine,
Bridges of understanding, a love so divine.

So let us embrace, with open hearts wide,
Each bridge that we build, let compassion be our guide.
In the tapestry woven with empathy's grace,
Bridges of understanding, our sacred space.

Through valleys and peaks, hand in hand we explore,
The bridges we've built are forever, encore.
With every connection, we forge and we stand,
Bridges of understanding, a united land.

In the Glow of Togetherness

In the evening light, we stand so close,
Whispers of dreams, where our hearts engross.
Hand in hand, we chase the dusk,
Bound by love, in every husk.

Laughter echoes, the stars align,
In your gaze, the world feels fine.
Every moment, a spark so bright,
Together forever, we face the night.

Through the storms, we find our way,
In the glow, forever we'll stay.
Your warmth, a beacon, guiding me,
In this bond, we are truly free.

With every heartbeat, we craft our tale,
In the darkest hours, we shall not pale.
In this embrace, we create our song,
In the glow of love, where we belong.

Together we rise, like the morning sun,
In the glow of togetherness, we've won.
Every breath shared, a treasure so rare,
In this journey together, nothing can compare.

A Palette of Memories

Brush strokes of laughter, colors of glee,
Each memory captured, hints of you and me.
Splashes of joy paint the canvas wide,
In the art of our journey, love is our guide.

Moments like sunsets, fading to night,
Vivid reflections in soft, golden light.
With every hue, we merge and blend,
In this palette of life, love will not end.

Dances in rain, whispers in shade,
Every moment together, sweetly portrayed.
In this vibrant mosaic, our hearts intertwine,
Crafting a masterpiece, divine and fine.

Like seasons that change, we evolve and grow,
Textures of life create ebb and flow.
In each brush stroke, stories unroll,
A palette of memories, forever our role.

Through laughter and tears, we sketch our fate,
In this art of together, we celebrate.
With every memory, a treasure to find,
A palette of love, uniquely designed.

Navigating Together's Map

In the still of night, we trace the stars,
Navigating dreams, no distance too far.
With every step, our paths align,
In this journey together, love will shine.

From winding roads to open skies,
With you by my side, I can truly rise.
Through valleys deep and mountains tall,
Our spirits entwined, we'll never fall.

Holding the compass, your hand in mine,
Guided by whispers of love's design.
Each bend in the road brings us near,
In navigating together, we conquer fear.

Through calm and tempest, our sails unfurled,
In the ocean of life, together we're twirled.
With laughter as our anchor, hope our map,
We'll chart our course, through every gap.

In this dance of time, let's chart the skies,
With every heartbeat, the adventure lies.
Navigating together, forever we roam,
In this vast world, we've found our home.

The Symphony of Us

In the quiet dawn, our music plays,
Notes of our laughter fill the days.
Each heartbeat a rhythm, each sigh a song,
In the symphony of us, where we belong.

Chords of connection, vibrant and true,
Melodies woven, just me and you.
Through highs and lows, we dance in tune,
In the concert of life, under the moon.

With every glance, we compose our score,
In the silence, there's so much more.
Harmony whispers in the calm of night,
Together we shine, two stars in flight.

As time keeps ticking, our music evolves,
In this grand opus, love always resolves.
With passion and grace, we share this dream,
In the symphony of us, we reign supreme.

In every encore, we rise once again,
With laughter and love, we'll never refrain.
In this beautiful journey, let's sing and trust,
For forever we'll play, in the symphony of us.

The Essence of Togetherness

In laughter we find our way,
Each moment a tender display.
Hearts intertwined, a sacred space,
Together we dance at our own pace.

Hand in hand through thick and thin,
With you by my side, we begin.
The world melts away in your eyes,
Together we reach for the skies.

Shared dreams whisper soft and clear,
Your presence alone brings me cheer.
Through storms and sunshine we roam,
In your heart, I find my home.

Every smile, a silent vow,
In moments fleeting, we live now.
Unified, we face each test,
In togetherness, we are blessed.

With every heartbeat, every sigh,
In this bond, together we fly.
Forever stitched in time's own thread,
The essence of love we both spread.

Embracing the Silence

In quiet moments, words are few,
Yet in this hush, I find you.
The calmness wraps like a warm embrace,
In silence, we share our sacred space.

A glance that speaks without a sound,
In this gentle stillness, we are found.
The comfort of presence, slow and deep,
In this tranquil moment, we safely keep.

Not every thought needs to take flight,
In the silence, everything feels right.
Together, we breathe, a silent song,
In our shared quiet, we both belong.

The hush of night, the dawn's soft glow,
In silence, our love continues to flow.
Through unspoken dreams and echoes of grace,
We find our rhythm, our perfect pace.

With every heartbeat, whispers draw near,
In the stillness, your heart I hear.
Together, in silence, our spirits soar,
In this embrace, we need nothing more.

The Melody of Us

In harmony, our spirits rise,
A chorus sung beneath the skies.
Each note a thread, woven tight,
In the melody, we find our light.

Your laughter dances through the air,
A symphony that we both share.
With every heartbeat, the song plays on,
Together we sing, forever drawn.

Through highs and lows, we find the tune,
In twilight's glow and afternoon.
The rhythm of love, steady and true,
In the melody, it's just me and you.

Let the world swirl, let the music sway,
In this embrace, we drift away.
With every whisper, every sigh,
In our melody, we soar high.

As seasons change, the song stays near,
In every note, I hold you dear.
A timeless harmony, we compose,
In the melody of us, love grows.

Rays of Shared Sunshine

In morning light, our laughter glows,
With every moment, the warmth grows.
Golden rays wrapped in embrace,
Together we shine in this sacred space.

Through clouds that gather, storms that sway,
We find the light in every day.
In the shadows, your smile breaks,
Each shared laugh, a heart that wakes.

Every sunset, a canvas bright,
With colors blending, a pure delight.
In our joy, the world feels right,
Rays of sunshine, a beautiful sight.

Through trials faced, hand in hand,
In love's warm glow, we take our stand.
Together we radiate, fiercely free,
In every heartbeat, just you and me.

With shared sunshine lighting our ways,
We find the magic in simple days.
In every touch, the warmth we gain,
Together forever, through joy and pain.

Garden of Shared Secrets

In whispers soft, we plant our dreams,
Among the flowers, where sunlight beams.
Each secret shared, a tender seed,
Growing in trust, a gentle creed.

Under the leaves, we find our space,
A haven rich with love's embrace.
Each bloom a tale, each root a bond,
Together we flourish, growing beyond.

In shades of green, our stories blend,
A symphony of joy, around each bend.
The petals dance in the morning light,
A garden of hope, forever bright.

As seasons change and time moves on,
The memories linger, like a soft song.
With every harvest, we gather near,
In this sacred place, our hearts sincere.

So let us wander, hand in hand,
In this garden of secrets, a promised land.
With every breath, we cultivate
A love that blooms, a shared fate.

A Mosaic of Shared Light

Each fragment shines, a story to tell,
In hues of laughter, we weave our spell.
Colors collide, and spirits align,
A tapestry bright, where hearts entwine.

With every shard, a whisper of grace,
Together we paint, our sacred space.
The light reflects, in shimmered dreams,
A mosaic formed by love's gentle beams.

Through shadows cast, we find our way,
In every dusk, there's a promise of day.
Each moment cherished, like stars in the night,
Together we shine, in harmony bright.

As hands join together, creation unfolds,
A symphony sung, as the future molds.
In every crack, a glimmer of hope,
Through trials faced, together we cope.

This mosaic of life, crafted with care,
Reminds us always, our love we share.
In every piece, a journey so true,
A canvas of light, painted by me and you.

The Safe Harbor We Build

With sturdy walls and open hearts,
We craft a place where love imparts.
Waves of life may crash and roar,
Yet in our harbor, we stand shore.

Each timber laid, a trust we lay,
In every shelter, hope holds sway.
The storms may come, but here we stand,
In the strength of unity, hand in hand.

A lighthouse shines, our guiding light,
In darkest times, it burns so bright.
Through winds of change, we will not part,
For in this harbor, beats one heart.

Together we weather, together we thrive,
In the warmth of love, we stay alive.
With anchors deep, we brace for all,
In this safe harbor, we shall not fall.

So here's to us, in calm and gale,
A story woven in every tale.
With laughter, joy, and dreams fulfilled,
This is the safe harbor we build.

Stories Woven in Laughter

In every chuckle, a story unfolds,
Of moments shared, both warm and bold.
Around the fire, we gather near,
In the laughter's echo, our spirits cheer.

Each tale a thread, in a rich tapestry,
Binding our hearts in sweet harmony.
With every smile, a memory we create,
In the fabric of time, love holds weight.

Through joyful whispers, we celebrate,
The bonds we've formed, they resonate.
With every giggle, we chase the gray,
In the stories shared, we find our way.

Though life's a journey with ups and downs,
In laughter's embrace, we shed our frowns.
In the joy we share, may we always find,
A refuge of warmth, a love intertwined.

So let us cherish, these moments bright,
In the stories we weave, our guiding light.
With laughter as our greatest art,
We share our lives, each other's heart.

Bonds Beyond the Horizon

In distant lands where shadows play,
Our hearts entwined, we find our way.
Through mountains high and rivers wide,
Together still, we bide our time.

The sun may set, the stars may rise,
Yet in your gaze, my solace lies.
With every breath, a whisper shared,
A bond unbroken, a love declared.

Though storms may come and winds may roar,
We stand as one, forevermore.
Each challenge faced, a story spun,
In unity, we have just begun.

Across the sea, your voice I hear,
A melody that draws me near.
With every step, our paths align,
In joy and sorrow, your heart is mine.

So let us dream beyond the night,
With hope and love as our guiding light.
For in this life, our souls will dance,
In bonds beyond, we take our chance.

In the Embrace of Laughter

In fields of gold, we dance and sway,
With laughter bright to light the way.
Each chuckle shared, a secret told,
In joy's warm arms, our spirits hold.

Through fleeting days, the moments blend,
In every smile, we find a friend.
The echoes of our love resound,
In gentle whispers, joy is found.

Under the stars, our dreams take flight,
In shared delight, the world feels right.
With every giggle, worries cease,
In laughter's hug, we find our peace.

So let us weave this tapestry,
Of joy and dreams, of you and me.
In cherished moments, let's believe,
In the embrace of laughter, we achieve.

For life is sweet, a fleeting dance,
In every heartbeat, a second chance.
Together always, hand in hand,
In love and laughter, we will stand.

Threads of Connection

In whispered words, our spirits weave,
A tapestry of dreams we believe.
Through tangled paths, we find our way,
In threads of connection, come what may.

With every heartbeat, stories unfold,
In shared moments, our hearts are bold.
The fabric of life, rich and bright,
In unity, we find our light.

Though distances stretch and silence reigns,
The bond we share forever remains.
Through whispered hopes and gentle sighs,
Our souls entwined, they never die.

In laughter's warmth and sorrow's tears,
We stitch together through the years.
For every journey, every flight,
Threads of connection hold us tight.

So let us cherish this woven art,
In every corner of the heart.
For in this web, we are complete,
In threads of love, our lives repeat.

When Hearts Align

In quiet moments, our hearts align,
Like stars that shimmer, a perfect sign.
With each soft glance, an understanding,
In silent echoes, love is commanding.

Through winding paths, we dare to roam,
In each other's eyes, we find our home.
With open arms, we greet the day,
As dreams unfold in a vibrant display.

The world may change, its seasons shift,
Yet in your heart, I find my gift.
Together we rise, two souls as one,
In love's warm glow, our journey's begun.

With every heartbeat, a rhythm sweet,
In harmony, our lives compete.
Through storms we weather, through trials we shine,
Forever blessed when hearts align.

In laughter shared and tears embraced,
Our love's reflection, time cannot waste.
So hand in hand, let's face the climb,
For when hearts align, it's always prime.

Milton Keynes UK
Ingram Content Group UK Ltd.
UKHW022142111124
451073UK00007B/153